# 50 Creative Brunch Recipe Ideas

By: Kelly Johnson

# Table of Contents

- Avocado Toast with Poached Egg
- Lemon Ricotta Pancakes
- Smoked Salmon Eggs Benedict
- Churro Waffles
- Croissant French Toast Bake
- Shakshuka with Feta
- Breakfast Tacos with Chorizo
- Sweet Potato Hash with Fried Eggs
- Blueberry Buttermilk Biscuits
- Spinach and Feta Frittata
- Peanut Butter and Banana Pancakes
- Bacon and Cheddar Scones
- Savory Oatmeal with Mushrooms
- Maple Pecan Sticky Buns
- Baked Apple Cinnamon Oatmeal
- Breakfast Quesadilla with Avocado
- Everything Bagel Breakfast Sandwich
- Carrot Cake Muffins
- Coconut Chia Pudding with Mango
- Breakfast Flatbread with Prosciutto
- Almond Croissant Bread Pudding
- Matcha Waffles with Berries
- Pumpkin Spice Donuts
- Kimchi Scrambled Eggs
- Strawberry Shortcake Pancakes
- Huevos Rancheros
- Italian Breakfast Skillet
- Caramelized Onion and Goat Cheese Tart
- Chocolate Chip Banana Bread French Toast
- Mediterranean Breakfast Wrap
- Brie and Cranberry Grilled Cheese
- Sourdough Avocado and Radish Toast
- Savory Herb and Cheese Dutch Baby
- Greek Yogurt Parfait with Granola
- Prosciutto-Wrapped Asparagus with Eggs

- Pineapple Upside-Down Pancakes
- Cornbread Waffles with Honey Butter
- Cacio e Pepe Scrambled Eggs
- Vegan Blueberry Lemon Scones
- Hash Brown Breakfast Pizza
- Caprese Breakfast Sandwich
- Blackberry and Basil Baked Oatmeal
- Smoked Gouda and Bacon Quiche
- Fig and Honey Ricotta Toast
- Green Smoothie Bowl with Almonds
- Zucchini and Corn Fritters
- S'mores Pancakes
- Maple Bacon Cinnamon Rolls
- Mediterranean Chickpea Scramble
- Cherry Almond Danish

## Avocado Toast with Poached Egg

**Ingredients:**

- 2 slices of sourdough bread, toasted
- 1 ripe avocado
- 2 eggs, poached
- ½ tsp lemon juice
- ¼ tsp salt
- ¼ tsp black pepper
- Red pepper flakes (optional)
- Fresh parsley or microgreens for garnish

**Instructions:**

1. Mash avocado with lemon juice, salt, and black pepper.
2. Spread avocado on toasted sourdough.
3. Top with a poached egg.
4. Garnish with red pepper flakes and parsley.

**Lemon Ricotta Pancakes**

**Ingredients:**

- 1 cup all-purpose flour
- 1 tsp baking powder
- ½ tsp baking soda
- ¼ tsp salt
- 2 tbsp sugar
- ¾ cup whole milk
- ½ cup ricotta cheese
- 1 egg
- 1 tbsp lemon zest
- 2 tbsp lemon juice
- ½ tsp vanilla extract
- Butter for cooking

**Instructions:**

1. Whisk flour, baking powder, baking soda, salt, and sugar.
2. In another bowl, mix milk, ricotta, egg, lemon zest, lemon juice, and vanilla.
3. Combine wet and dry ingredients until just mixed.
4. Cook pancakes over medium heat until golden brown.

## Smoked Salmon Eggs Benedict

**Ingredients:**

- 2 English muffins, split and toasted
- 4 slices smoked salmon
- 4 poached eggs
- 1 cup hollandaise sauce
- 1 tbsp chopped chives

**Instructions:**

1. Place smoked salmon on toasted English muffins.
2. Top each with a poached egg.
3. Drizzle with hollandaise sauce and sprinkle with chives.

**Churro Waffles**

**Ingredients:**

- 2 cups waffle mix
- 1 ¼ cups milk
- 2 eggs
- 1 tsp cinnamon
- ¼ cup melted butter
- ½ cup sugar

**Instructions:**

1. Prepare waffle batter according to package instructions. Add cinnamon.
2. Cook waffles until golden.
3. Brush with melted butter and sprinkle with sugar.

**Croissant French Toast Bake**

**Ingredients:**

- 4 croissants, torn into pieces
- 3 eggs
- 1 cup milk
- ¼ cup heavy cream
- ¼ cup sugar
- 1 tsp vanilla
- ½ tsp cinnamon

**Instructions:**

1. Preheat oven to 350°F.
2. Whisk eggs, milk, cream, sugar, vanilla, and cinnamon.
3. Pour over croissants in a baking dish.
4. Bake for 25 minutes.

**Shakshuka with Feta**

**Ingredients:**

- 1 tbsp olive oil
- 1 small onion, chopped
- 1 bell pepper, chopped
- 3 cloves garlic, minced
- 1 can (14.5 oz) crushed tomatoes
- 1 tsp cumin
- ½ tsp paprika
- ½ tsp salt
- 4 eggs
- ¼ cup feta cheese

**Instructions:**

1. Sauté onion and bell pepper in olive oil.
2. Add garlic, tomatoes, and spices. Simmer for 10 minutes.
3. Make 4 wells and crack in eggs. Cover and cook for 5 minutes.
4. Sprinkle with feta and serve.

## Breakfast Tacos with Chorizo

**Ingredients:**

- 4 small tortillas
- ½ lb chorizo, cooked
- 4 scrambled eggs
- ½ cup shredded cheese
- ¼ cup salsa
- ¼ cup chopped cilantro

**Instructions:**

1. Fill tortillas with chorizo and eggs.
2. Top with cheese, salsa, and cilantro.

**Sweet Potato Hash with Fried Eggs**

**Ingredients:**

- 1 large sweet potato, diced
- ½ onion, chopped
- 1 bell pepper, chopped
- 2 eggs
- 1 tbsp olive oil

**Instructions:**

1. Sauté sweet potato, onion, and bell pepper in olive oil.
2. Cook for 10 minutes until tender.
3. Fry eggs and serve on top.

## Blueberry Buttermilk Biscuits

**Ingredients:**

- 2 cups flour
- 1 tbsp sugar
- 1 tsp baking powder
- ½ tsp baking soda
- ½ tsp salt
- ½ cup cold butter, cubed
- ¾ cup buttermilk
- ½ cup blueberries

**Instructions:**

1. Mix dry ingredients, then cut in butter.
2. Add buttermilk and blueberries.
3. Bake at 400°F for 15 minutes.

**Spinach and Feta Frittata**

**Ingredients:**

- 6 eggs
- ½ cup milk
- 1 cup spinach, chopped
- ½ cup feta cheese
- 1 tbsp olive oil

**Instructions:**

1. Preheat oven to 375°F.
2. Sauté spinach in olive oil.
3. Whisk eggs and milk. Pour into a pan.
4. Sprinkle with feta and bake for 20 minutes.

# Peanut Butter and Banana Pancakes

**Ingredients:**

- 1 cup all-purpose flour
- 1 tsp baking powder
- ½ tsp baking soda
- ¼ tsp salt
- 1 tbsp sugar
- 1 ripe banana, mashed
- 1 egg
- ¾ cup milk
- 2 tbsp peanut butter, melted
- ½ tsp vanilla extract
- Butter for cooking

**Instructions:**

1. Whisk flour, baking powder, baking soda, salt, and sugar.
2. In another bowl, mix mashed banana, egg, milk, peanut butter, and vanilla.
3. Combine wet and dry ingredients.
4. Cook pancakes over medium heat until golden brown.
5. Serve with extra peanut butter and banana slices.

## Bacon and Cheddar Scones

**Ingredients:**

- 2 cups all-purpose flour
- 1 tbsp baking powder
- ½ tsp salt
- ½ cup cold butter, cubed
- 1 cup shredded cheddar cheese
- ½ cup cooked, crumbled bacon
- ¾ cup heavy cream

**Instructions:**

1. Preheat oven to 400°F.
2. Mix flour, baking powder, and salt.
3. Cut in butter until the mixture resembles crumbs.
4. Fold in cheese and bacon, then add cream.
5. Form dough into a circle, cut into wedges, and bake for 15-18 minutes.

## Savory Oatmeal with Mushrooms

### Ingredients:

- 1 cup rolled oats
- 2 cups vegetable broth
- ½ cup mushrooms, sliced
- 1 garlic clove, minced
- 1 tbsp olive oil
- ½ tsp salt
- ½ tsp black pepper
- 1 soft-boiled egg (optional)

### Instructions:

1. Cook oats in vegetable broth.
2. Sauté mushrooms and garlic in olive oil.
3. Stir mushrooms into oats.
4. Top with a soft-boiled egg.

## Maple Pecan Sticky Buns

**Ingredients:**

- 1 sheet puff pastry
- ½ cup chopped pecans
- ¼ cup brown sugar
- 1 tsp cinnamon
- ¼ cup maple syrup
- 2 tbsp melted butter

**Instructions:**

1. Preheat oven to 375°F.
2. Mix pecans, brown sugar, and cinnamon.
3. Brush puff pastry with butter, sprinkle with mixture, and roll up.
4. Slice into buns, drizzle with maple syrup, and bake for 20 minutes.

## Baked Apple Cinnamon Oatmeal

**Ingredients:**

- 2 cups rolled oats
- 1 tsp cinnamon
- ½ tsp nutmeg
- 1 apple, diced
- 2 cups milk
- ¼ cup maple syrup
- 1 egg, beaten

**Instructions:**

1. Preheat oven to 350°F.
2. Mix all ingredients in a bowl.
3. Pour into a baking dish and bake for 30 minutes.

## Breakfast Quesadilla with Avocado

**Ingredients:**

- 2 large tortillas
- 2 scrambled eggs
- ½ avocado, sliced
- ½ cup shredded cheese
- ¼ cup salsa

**Instructions:**

1. Fill tortilla with eggs, avocado, and cheese.
2. Fold and cook in a skillet until crispy.
3. Serve with salsa.

# Everything Bagel Breakfast Sandwich

**Ingredients:**

- 1 everything bagel, toasted
- 1 fried egg
- 2 slices bacon
- 1 tbsp cream cheese
- 1 slice tomato

**Instructions:**

1. Spread cream cheese on the bagel.
2. Layer egg, bacon, and tomato.

**Carrot Cake Muffins**

**Ingredients:**

- 1 ½ cups flour
- 1 tsp baking soda
- ½ tsp salt
- 1 tsp cinnamon
- ½ cup sugar
- ½ cup grated carrots
- ½ cup applesauce
- 1 egg

**Instructions:**

1. Preheat oven to 350°F.
2. Mix all ingredients.
3. Pour into muffin tin and bake for 20 minutes.

# Coconut Chia Pudding with Mango

**Ingredients:**

- ½ cup chia seeds
- 2 cups coconut milk
- 1 tbsp honey
- ½ cup diced mango

**Instructions:**

1. Mix chia seeds, coconut milk, and honey.
2. Refrigerate overnight.
3. Top with mango before serving.

## Breakfast Flatbread with Prosciutto

**Ingredients:**

- 1 flatbread or naan
- 2 tbsp olive oil
- ½ cup shredded mozzarella
- 2 slices prosciutto
- 1 egg
- ¼ tsp black pepper
- ¼ tsp red pepper flakes
- Fresh arugula for garnish

**Instructions:**

1. Preheat oven to 400°F.
2. Brush flatbread with olive oil, sprinkle with mozzarella.
3. Crack egg onto the flatbread and bake for 10-12 minutes.
4. Top with prosciutto, black pepper, red pepper flakes, and arugula.

## Almond Croissant Bread Pudding

**Ingredients:**

- 4 croissants, torn into pieces
- 1 cup milk
- 1 cup heavy cream
- 3 eggs
- ½ cup sugar
- 1 tsp vanilla extract
- ½ cup sliced almonds
- Powdered sugar for garnish

**Instructions:**

1. Preheat oven to 350°F.
2. Whisk milk, cream, eggs, sugar, and vanilla.
3. Pour over croissants in a baking dish.
4. Sprinkle with almonds and bake for 35-40 minutes.
5. Dust with powdered sugar before serving.

## Matcha Waffles with Berries

**Ingredients:**

- 1 ½ cups flour
- 1 tbsp matcha powder
- 1 tbsp sugar
- 1 tsp baking powder
- ½ tsp salt
- 1 cup milk
- 1 egg
- ¼ cup melted butter
- Mixed berries for topping

**Instructions:**

1. Preheat waffle iron.
2. Mix flour, matcha, sugar, baking powder, and salt.
3. In another bowl, whisk milk, egg, and butter.
4. Combine and cook in waffle iron.
5. Serve with berries and syrup.

## Pumpkin Spice Donuts

**Ingredients:**

- 1 ½ cups flour
- 1 tsp baking powder
- ½ tsp salt
- 1 tsp cinnamon
- ½ tsp nutmeg
- ½ cup sugar
- ½ cup pumpkin puree
- 1 egg
- ¼ cup milk

**Instructions:**

1. Preheat oven to 375°F.
2. Mix dry ingredients in one bowl, wet in another.
3. Combine and pipe into a donut pan.
4. Bake for 12-15 minutes.
5. Roll in cinnamon sugar before serving.

**Kimchi Scrambled Eggs**

**Ingredients:**

- 3 eggs
- ¼ cup kimchi, chopped
- 1 tbsp butter
- ¼ tsp soy sauce
- 1 green onion, sliced

**Instructions:**

1. Heat butter in a pan, add kimchi, and cook for 2 minutes.
2. Whisk eggs with soy sauce and pour in.
3. Scramble gently until cooked.
4. Garnish with green onions.

## Strawberry Shortcake Pancakes

**Ingredients:**

- 1 cup flour
- 1 tbsp sugar
- 1 tsp baking powder
- ½ tsp salt
- ¾ cup milk
- 1 egg
- ½ tsp vanilla
- ½ cup sliced strawberries
- Whipped cream for topping

**Instructions:**

1. Mix dry ingredients.
2. In another bowl, whisk milk, egg, and vanilla.
3. Combine and cook pancakes until golden brown.
4. Layer with strawberries and whipped cream.

**Huevos Rancheros**

**Ingredients:**

- 2 tortillas
- 2 eggs
- ½ cup black beans
- ½ cup salsa
- ¼ cup crumbled queso fresco
- 1 tbsp olive oil

**Instructions:**

1. Heat tortillas in a skillet.
2. Fry eggs in olive oil.
3. Top tortillas with eggs, black beans, salsa, and cheese.

## Italian Breakfast Skillet

**Ingredients:**

- 2 Italian sausages, sliced
- ½ cup cherry tomatoes, halved
- ½ cup diced potatoes
- 2 eggs
- ¼ cup shredded Parmesan
- 1 tbsp olive oil

**Instructions:**

1. Heat oil in a skillet and cook potatoes.
2. Add sausage and tomatoes, cook until browned.
3. Make wells in the skillet and crack in eggs.
4. Cook until eggs set, then sprinkle with Parmesan.

# Caramelized Onion and Goat Cheese Tart

**Ingredients:**

- 1 sheet puff pastry
- 1 large onion, sliced
- 2 tbsp butter
- ½ cup goat cheese
- 1 egg, beaten
- 1 tsp thyme

**Instructions:**

1. Preheat oven to 375°F.
2. Sauté onions in butter until golden.
3. Spread onto puff pastry, top with goat cheese and thyme.
4. Brush edges with egg wash and bake for 20 minutes.

# Chocolate Chip Banana Bread French Toast

**Ingredients:**

- 2 slices banana bread
- 1 egg
- ¼ cup milk
- ½ tsp cinnamon
- ¼ cup chocolate chips
- Butter for cooking

**Instructions:**

1. Whisk egg, milk, and cinnamon.
2. Dip banana bread and cook in buttered skillet.
3. Sprinkle with chocolate chips and serve.

**Mediterranean Breakfast Wrap**

**Ingredients:**

- 1 whole wheat tortilla
- 2 scrambled eggs
- ¼ cup cherry tomatoes, diced
- ¼ cup cucumber, diced
- 2 tbsp feta cheese
- 2 tbsp hummus
- ¼ tsp oregano

**Instructions:**

1. Spread hummus on tortilla.
2. Add scrambled eggs, tomatoes, cucumber, and feta.
3. Sprinkle with oregano, wrap, and serve.

## Brie and Cranberry Grilled Cheese

**Ingredients:**

- 2 slices sourdough bread
- 3 oz brie cheese, sliced
- 2 tbsp cranberry sauce
- 1 tbsp butter

**Instructions:**

1. Butter one side of each bread slice.
2. Layer brie and cranberry sauce between bread.
3. Grill in a pan until golden brown and cheese melts.

## Sourdough Avocado and Radish Toast

**Ingredients:**

- 1 slice sourdough bread
- ½ avocado, mashed
- 2 radishes, thinly sliced
- ½ tsp lemon juice
- Pinch of sea salt

**Instructions:**

1. Toast the sourdough.
2. Spread mashed avocado on top.
3. Add radishes, lemon juice, and salt.

## Savory Herb and Cheese Dutch Baby

**Ingredients:**

- 3 eggs
- ½ cup milk
- ½ cup flour
- ½ tsp salt
- ½ tsp dried thyme
- ¼ cup shredded Gruyère cheese

**Instructions:**

1. Preheat oven to 425°F with a cast-iron skillet inside.
2. Blend eggs, milk, flour, salt, and thyme.
3. Melt butter in the hot skillet, pour batter in.
4. Sprinkle cheese on top and bake for 15-18 minutes.

## Greek Yogurt Parfait with Granola

**Ingredients:**

- 1 cup Greek yogurt
- ½ cup granola
- ¼ cup mixed berries
- 1 tsp honey

**Instructions:**

1. Layer Greek yogurt, granola, and berries in a glass.
2. Drizzle with honey before serving.

## Prosciutto-Wrapped Asparagus with Eggs

**Ingredients:**

- 6 asparagus spears
- 3 slices prosciutto
- 2 eggs
- 1 tbsp olive oil

**Instructions:**

1. Wrap asparagus with prosciutto and roast at 400°F for 10 minutes.
2. Fry eggs and serve over asparagus.

## Pineapple Upside-Down Pancakes

**Ingredients:**

- 1 cup pancake mix
- ½ cup milk
- 1 egg
- ½ tsp vanilla extract
- 4 pineapple rings
- 2 tbsp brown sugar
- 1 tbsp butter

**Instructions:**

1. Prepare pancake batter.
2. Melt butter in a skillet, add brown sugar and pineapple rings.
3. Pour batter over pineapple and cook until golden.

## Cornbread Waffles with Honey Butter

**Ingredients:**

- 1 cup cornbread mix
- ½ cup milk
- 1 egg
- 2 tbsp melted butter
- 2 tbsp honey

**Instructions:**

1. Mix cornbread batter and cook in a waffle iron.
2. Mix melted butter with honey and drizzle over waffles.

**Cacio e Pepe Scrambled Eggs**

**Ingredients:**

- 3 eggs
- 1 tbsp butter
- 2 tbsp grated Pecorino Romano
- ½ tsp black pepper

**Instructions:**

1. Whisk eggs and cook in butter over low heat.
2. Stir in cheese and black pepper before serving.

## Vegan Blueberry Lemon Scones

**Ingredients:**

- 2 cups flour
- ½ cup coconut oil
- ½ cup almond milk
- ¼ cup sugar
- 1 tbsp lemon zest
- ½ cup blueberries
- 1 tbsp baking powder

**Instructions:**

1. Preheat oven to 375°F.
2. Mix dry ingredients, add coconut oil and almond milk.
3. Fold in blueberries, shape dough into a circle, cut into wedges.
4. Bake for 20 minutes.

## Hash Brown Breakfast Pizza

**Ingredients:**

- 2 cups frozen hash browns
- 2 eggs
- ½ cup shredded cheese
- ¼ cup diced bell peppers
- 2 tbsp olive oil

**Instructions:**

1. Preheat oven to 400°F.
2. Press hash browns into a greased pan to form a crust.
3. Bake for 15 minutes, add toppings and bake for 10 more minutes.

## Caprese Breakfast Sandwich

**Ingredients:**

- 1 English muffin or ciabatta roll
- 1 egg, fried or scrambled
- 2 slices fresh mozzarella
- 2 tomato slices
- 3 fresh basil leaves
- 1 tbsp pesto
- 1 tsp balsamic glaze

**Instructions:**

1. Toast the English muffin.
2. Spread pesto on both halves.
3. Layer egg, mozzarella, tomato, and basil.
4. Drizzle with balsamic glaze and serve.

# Blackberry and Basil Baked Oatmeal

**Ingredients:**

- 2 cups rolled oats
- 1 tsp baking powder
- ½ tsp cinnamon
- ¼ tsp salt
- 1 ½ cups almond milk
- 1 egg
- ¼ cup honey or maple syrup
- ½ tsp vanilla extract
- 1 cup blackberries
- 2 tbsp chopped fresh basil

**Instructions:**

1. Preheat oven to 375°F.
2. Mix oats, baking powder, cinnamon, and salt.
3. In another bowl, whisk milk, egg, honey, and vanilla.
4. Combine with oat mixture, fold in blackberries and basil.
5. Pour into a greased dish and bake for 30 minutes.

## Smoked Gouda and Bacon Quiche

**Ingredients:**

- 1 pie crust
- 6 eggs
- 1 cup milk
- 1 cup shredded smoked gouda
- ½ cup cooked bacon, crumbled
- ¼ cup chopped green onions
- ¼ tsp black pepper

**Instructions:**

1. Preheat oven to 375°F.
2. Whisk eggs, milk, and pepper.
3. Pour into the pie crust, sprinkle with cheese, bacon, and green onions.
4. Bake for 35-40 minutes until set.

## Fig and Honey Ricotta Toast

**Ingredients:**

- 1 slice sourdough bread, toasted
- ¼ cup ricotta cheese
- 2 fresh figs, sliced
- 1 tsp honey
- ¼ tsp cinnamon

**Instructions:**

1. Spread ricotta on toast.
2. Top with fig slices.
3. Drizzle with honey and sprinkle with cinnamon.

## Green Smoothie Bowl with Almonds

**Ingredients:**

- 1 frozen banana
- ½ cup spinach
- ½ cup Greek yogurt
- ½ cup almond milk
- 1 tbsp almond butter
- 1 tbsp honey
- ¼ cup sliced almonds (for topping)
- ¼ cup granola (for topping)

**Instructions:**

1. Blend banana, spinach, yogurt, almond milk, almond butter, and honey.
2. Pour into a bowl and top with almonds and granola.

## Zucchini and Corn Fritters

**Ingredients:**

- 1 zucchini, grated and drained
- ½ cup corn kernels
- ¼ cup grated Parmesan
- ¼ cup flour
- 1 egg
- ½ tsp salt
- ¼ tsp black pepper
- 1 tbsp olive oil

**Instructions:**

1. Mix all ingredients in a bowl.
2. Heat oil in a pan, scoop batter, and flatten into patties.
3. Cook for 3-4 minutes per side until golden brown.

## S'mores Pancakes

**Ingredients:**

- 1 cup pancake mix
- ½ cup milk
- 1 egg
- ¼ tsp vanilla extract
- ¼ cup crushed graham crackers
- ¼ cup chocolate chips
- ¼ cup mini marshmallows

**Instructions:**

1. Prepare pancake batter and mix in graham crackers.
2. Cook pancakes, then top with chocolate chips and marshmallows.
3. Use a torch or broil in the oven for 1 minute to melt marshmallows.

## Maple Bacon Cinnamon Rolls

**Ingredients:**

- 1 can refrigerated cinnamon rolls
- 6 slices bacon, cooked and crumbled
- ¼ cup maple syrup

**Instructions:**

1. Preheat oven and bake cinnamon rolls as directed.
2. Drizzle with maple syrup and top with bacon crumbles.

**Mediterranean Chickpea Scramble**

**Ingredients:**

- ½ cup canned chickpeas, mashed
- 2 eggs
- ¼ cup cherry tomatoes, diced
- ¼ cup spinach, chopped
- 2 tbsp feta cheese
- 1 tsp olive oil

**Instructions:**

1. Heat oil in a pan and cook chickpeas for 2 minutes.
2. Add eggs and scramble.
3. Stir in tomatoes, spinach, and feta before serving.

# Cherry Almond Danish

**Ingredients:**

- 1 sheet puff pastry, thawed
- ½ cup cherry preserves
- ¼ cup sliced almonds
- 1 egg (for egg wash)
- 1 tbsp powdered sugar (for dusting)

**Instructions:**

1. Preheat oven to 375°F.
2. Cut puff pastry into rectangles, place cherry preserves in the center.
3. Fold edges over and brush with egg wash.
4. Sprinkle with almonds and bake for 20 minutes.
5. Dust with powdered sugar before serving.

www.ingramcontent.com/pod-product-compliance
Lightning Source LLC
LaVergne TN
LVHW081334060526
838201LV00055B/2645